TARANTELLA

Peter, I am so thankful
for your friendship, your
amazing poetry, and
your kindness.

Rebecca Loudon

Love,
Rebecca
12/1/04

Acknowledgements

I would like to thank the following publications in which some of these poems first appeared:

Anemone Sidecar, Arsenic Lobster, Avatar Review, Blue Fifth, Blue Monk Press, Borderlands: Texas Poetry Review, Can We Have Our Ball Back?, Crab Orchard Review, Fine Madness, Gumball Poetry, Literary Salt, Metro King County Poetry & Art on the Buses, Pacific Review, Pontoon 6, Portland Review, Rock Salt Plum, Seattle Review, Snakeskin, Snow Monkey, Spindrift, Square Lake, Stride Magazine, Switched-on Gutenberg, Taverner's Koans, and *Wicked Alice.*

Special thanks to the Wallingford Irregulars Poetry Workshop for supplying me with poems to read, friendship and a reason to bake bread, the Nine Poets Poetry Workshop for their support and help on many of these poems, the Jack Straw Writers program, the Shakarian Foundation, and to Page Loudon for his keen eye, his quick sense of humor and his willingness, always, to listen.

Published by Ravenna Press
PO Box 127, Edmonds, WA 98020
Printed in the United States
All Rights Reserved
ISBN: 0-9723329-8-7

For Page

Table of Contents

The Bite

The Dance

The Cure

tarantella

\Tar`an*tel"la\, n. [It.] (Mus.) (a) A rapid and delirious sort of Neapolitan dance in 6-8 time, which moves in whirling triplets; — so called from a popular notion of its being a remedy against the poisonous bite of the tarantula. (b) Music suited to such a dance.

—*The American Heritage Dictionary of the English Language, Fourth Edition*

TARANTELLA

The Bite

Instructions for Recalcitrant Patients

Are you having a seizure?
I'm recovering from a spider bite
by embracing the tarantella; a low dance
in which I turn on my heels, snap my fingers and shuffle.

Do you know where you are?
During earthquakes, I cradle my violin
and regard the migration
of seabirds.

What is your name?
When Saint Dymphna was fifteen,
her father drew his sword and cut off her head.
Let us be inspired by her example
and comforted by her merciful help.
Amen.

What am I holding? (Hold up a common object such as a comb or watch.)
The ocean squalls down my chimney.
The power is out, my house cresting on its timbre.
I eat a jellyfish; swallow brine and chew,
a stinging sensation on my tongue.

Hold your arms straight out in front of you.
Will you remember, Rebecca, the way you rocked
in your chair when you played Schumann, the Rhein
covered in oil, burning?

Uncertain Geometry

She can't get out of the bookstore fast enough,
carries a volume of short stories and a recording
of symphonies by Schumann who had Eusebius
and Florestan arguing in his head and died
of anorexia in a German hospital.
She smells bacon frying. Fractals drift
from an inverted cone in front of her eyes.
Mandelbrot, but she can't find his name.
Bach plays in the telescoping corridor.
On the escalator, her great toe slips from her sandal,
peels open on the steel grid.
She wraps toilet paper around her foot to escape
without leaving a trail, she can make it to the car—
his name *Mandelbrot, Mandelbrot, The Mandelbrot Set*
pristine as a fugue flutters in her temporal lobe,
that ecstatic little ping, the aura of seizure.

At the Lucky Day Laundromat

Six turquoise chairs were welded
at the hip. The whole row moved
when Margaret nudged it with her foot.
She sat on the floor by her dryer,

watched the circle and fall of a striped
sock, rocked a bit, hugging her knees,
breathed the antiseptic scent of fabric
softener, bleach, shirts spread

like cormorants on green hangers,
the basket's tussle and squeak
as the attendant wheeled by scraping
lint from mesh screens.

Margaret wanted to burrow in warm
clothes; sheets, towels, trousers,
the shed skins of children.
She pressed her cheek against

the plastic door, then her mouth, flush
and open. She swallowed the servo hum,
ate motor, churn, cog and oil, the ping
of coins sliding home.

Duck God

Duane stands on Tadpole Pond bridge,
his grandfather's 1934 Herter's duck caller
tucked in the pocket of his down jacket.
He rubs the caller's amber tip, the worn
walnut body with its circular grooves.
Duane reaches into a plastic bag of oats,
sprinkles a handful to the ducks that skim
and dive. He finesses the ducks, lifts them
up and toward him with his calls; trumpet,
hiss, grunt, bark, squeak, cluck, coo.
Salt water seeps into Duane's rubber
boots, toes itching hot in wool socks.
He calls the ducks by name; mallard,
widgeon, green-winged teal, pintail,
merganser. The names feel smooth
in his mouth, like a lullaby. On calm
days they hear him for miles, wing in
to pluck bread from his fingers.

How Margaret Falls

She falls again, splayed on hands and knees
in the parking lot of the Italian restaurant.
In the car, she digs small stones from each palm,
the top of her left foot—
a botched stigmata.

It's like this, she says, *I got up too fast, dizzy
from gin in a glass thin enough to bite.*

She lights a cigarette, throws her ruined stocking out the window.
I lean across the steering wheel, lick *Brazen Raisin* lipstick
from her mouth, tongue her overlapping tooth.

*We are not,
we are not,
we are not what you think.*

Margaret presses fingers to eyes,
arches her foot once, twice, against the dashboard.

Blue Pill

Doctor tells me to continue the pills
I show her hands full of hair
skin pinched pink as boiled potatoes
tongue spooling out
She says *it's only been two months, give it a chance*

At night birds stand on my eyes
their prickled feet dig in
I dream of my dead, loudly
or wake every hour

I forget the names for things
drum
fountain
ribbon
key
She says *we can't have you crying on the bus*

Poetry hides there
under spoons and plates
the broken skein of thought
and too much food
Hides like a willful child
or a winter dog
and my son says
I like you better crazy

Rash

Every morning his wife leaned over the sink,
scraped burnt toast with the flat of a butter knife,
hips shifting inside a blue bathrobe knotted
tight as a Boy Scout's kerchief.

Schrack, schrack, schrack, schrack.
The noise cracked his skin. First, a blister
back of his knees, then his thighs splotched.
Crimson bloomed to groin, belly, palms, face.

He bathed in colloidal oats, slathered cortisone
and talc into the soft folds of his body.
The rash grew like a carapace; even the tiny curves
between his toes crusted and split.

He needed a poultice: sheets damped in river water,
milk-soaked bread twined to his trunk with gauze,
another skin against his, a great molting.

She said, *I can smell you from the other room,* pushed
his scaly hand from her breast, walked to the kitchen,
to her cups, bowls, spoons and plates, her sink
with its gleaming spigot, her slick, white oven.

St. Clare

When she stopped sleeping her eyelids rasped
like a child clacking animal bones together.
Her teeth were tight and slick as seeds.
Her skin broke apart and a dog
ate the fingers of her left hand.

She didn't leave her house for six hundred days,
spoke to no one. The painter abandoned her, crossed
his wrists in some sort of sign, did not kiss her salad mouth
as he backed out the door, shouting in Italian.

She built herself an aeroplane, self-cleaning cupboards, a club foot
She stared without medication into the green Mediterranean.
It was a miracle, of sorts, reported by a host of newspapers,
and the gift shop at the grotto carried tiny statues
of her likeness.

Tremor

Begin here: the index finger of my right hand twitching,
bony fish attached to hand, arm, elbow, shoulder cup
and ball, the stem of neck, my brain—
that faulty toy.

Begin here: he shaves my hair. I catch blonde clumps
as they fall. He opens my skull, presses with his thumb
here, here and here, brain coil wet and pulsing
like those black and white movies where hunched men
scoop and dig.

Begin here: Saturday mornings, across the street
from my mother's house. Frances Berry carries a cup of tea,
rattle-rattle-rattles her way from the kitchen, rice-paper napkins,
Prokofiev, the smell of turpentine and linseed oil.

Begin here: my brain's slick hive disconnected from its queen,
popping in spiky green lines. *What do you see when I push here?*
A knit hat, my pink shoes, stop, stop,
oh, such a pop.

Darlene Reads Her Future in Fortune Cookies

There is a problem with your foot, the left great toe, in particular.

Your toenail will be pierced with a needle heated in a gas flame.

You will learn the language of gangrene.

Your toe will be amputated at the first joint by a doctor with a small circular saw.

You will learn the language of morphine.

You will find work in a home for the aged in Sparks, Nevada, earning $4.37 an hour.

Eventually, your foot will stop aching.

Margaret Trims Her Wicks

Margaret has a plan for becoming famous
or at least knowing someone famous
or fucking someone famous. The details
aren't clear. She controls critical aspects

      1. dirt/mold along the window sill
      2. organized cupboards/closets
      3. under the sink
      4. bathtub rim
      5. something happened

She doesn't give a ratsass, she says, for men.
She cleans and cleans her house, hands rashy
with bleach. This has been her job for months.
That, and being sick

      1. eu-phe-mism

Margaret makes lists, thinks this might speed
things up. She listens to the police scanner
at night, all channels clear, squelch, dispatch
voice bringing crime live! into her house

      2. Ocean Charles X-Ray copy that
      3. suspect drives a dark blue Ford sedan
      4. woman finds her front door kicked open
      5. what happened in her bedroom what

It's not a very good plan. Margaret reads
all the latest how-to books but does not
follow directions clearly, does not meet
the required skill sets as stated
in her behavioral profile

> 6. nursing home aide
> 7. fry cook/mechanic
> 8. await further instructions
> 9. composite drawing/identify

Her face is beginning to wear. She still looks
young but the muscles around her mouth sag.
She hates this, wants to find a new face,
practices saying her name in the mirror
as she tweezes her eyebrows.

Warning Signs

Her name is Roxie. She is blonde, walks in film noir, drinks shots of tequila for breakfast, prefers garter belts to pantyhose. She is in love with beautiful shoes, lives alone.

Actually, her name is Margaret. Her hair is shit-blonde. She knows the 7 warning signs of seizure. She is telekinetic, smells gardenias and cigar smoke when she reads near fluorescent lights, thinks she can fly. She might head south for the winter.

No. Her name is Renate. She cooks chocolate torte, brioche, coq au vin, spiced pears. Her husband watches from behind the pantry door, watches, watches, groans, leans into his palm. Renate tips the roasting pan into the sink, lets the pink blood run out.

Her real name is Ruby. She takes Tegretol with port for lunch, writes illustrated children's books about car crashes where the mother is drunk and the child flies through the windshield. She rubs the bruise that presses into her temporal lobe, pets it like a cat, pets and pets it like a darling cat.

Stutter

That you could
tuck the curve
curved neck
goose's neck
down forcefully
to the side
open it open
sleek arch
you are prepared
pared.
Oh no love,
no, oh not
you said
it's kill
it's killing me.
Goose head
black beak
skewered
on a branch!
I slip
slip the knot
in a champagne
dress,
exposed
expose
where your tongue
your tongue lives
oh beautiful
liar.

What She Found in the Night Garden

Wick
She was bound to him by a length of surgical wick curled into her ear, soft-spun cotton thread used to draw the burning liquid up and out, a braid tucked into the helix, the drum-shaped shell, the spindle, tail floating on top to carry moisture away as from the heart, a capillary attraction. She needed a scaled diagram, detailed instructions of the procedure to stop the thing that spilled out of her, that soaked her hair, a sponge, a drain, something to draw the wetness that woke her at night covered in water as a thing the sea spit up, a thing the sea gave back as faulty, too full of salt, too full of heat.

Root
She raises gardenias in the bathroom of the red hotel, pinches milky blooms, their scent spilling out, plucks at the root, rubs slick leaves. He takes the stairs three at a time, *hurry*, turns the brass knob as she sings to flower, steam, sky, fills the claw-foot tub whose feet point west, sea sloshing up the sides. He wants to still her, covers her mouth with his hand, *shhh, shhh*. Cormorants spread their ragged wing on the pilings, goose, osprey, heron, swallow the air. She wants to fix everything; black mold on leaves, porch swing, cracked cup on the counter, whispering children. She bends her face to the tub, steam rising, tumbling, pulls him to the water, says *here then, here.*

Sting

The bee enters her humming along the edge of her nerve, yellow black body fat with sugar, fine fur stirring under her finger, tightly folded tongue tunneling out to suck, to gather, the thick barbed stinger that could strike (but does not) the mouth that could bite (but does not.) She drops to her knees in the garden when he leaves (in this story he always leaves.) She cannot let him go (she always lets him go) humming back to the hive, back to the queen in her comb, all that gold pouring from his body.

Aviary

She lives now with stutters & whores
just as her grandfather predicted,
    [fire eater, human blockhead, bed of nails]

watches the neighbor's window dim
or festive at dusk, drinks a bit more wine
each day, empties the bottle by six,
speaks her father's language the closer
she gets to affection, to *drunk*,
    [appellation d'origine, cru classé, vin de pays]

finds owls in the cupboard or gripping
the towel rack in the bathroom, asks
them to leave, uses a polite voice, open
vowels. Her chair scoots three inches to the left
every night & bites her wrist when she sits
    [blind bite, jewel line, torn cloud]

thinking *earthquake*, the floor thumping up
like a fist and she shivers, gold and red,
folded into herself, belly full
of hummingbirds.

Margaret Watches *The Misfits*

It's the way Marilyn's mouth moves;
upper lip swabbing her teeth,
a constant undulation.
Her long breasts slope,
loose against the white blouse,
its little darts tucked
for women without breasts.

Margaret unravels the fringe
on her bedspread one braid at a time,
fanning the frizzed yarn.
In a year she has made it nearly half
way around. She sips port from a child's
plastic cup, hair a brown scrub.
All that Nevada dust presses
into her clothes, pushing, insisting.

Clark Gable's paunch sloops
under his cowboy shirt, new jeans
pulled up to his chest. Eli Wallach
pumps his fat, clumsy legs against
Marilyn's ass. Margaret pours
another cup of port as they suck
at the blonde's mouth, lift her
off the porch, their white arms
soft as bread.

The mustangs kick and jerk
at Margaret's ribs. Hooves,
sharp blades, pummel her heart.
She curls fists against stomach,
dry hair wisping as she leans
toward the floor to smooth
the bedspread with her hands.

Wendy's Lament

where are you boy the figs loose
their sugar and night is worst of all
cats pull pins from voodoo dolls
trees press knobby hands down
my satin down my satin dress you
fly-by boy you dog-bit fish-mouth
radio flyer boy crow at my window
all eyes and hands your slick stick
shaking quick my father's here fall
like honey into the fluttering peach
pit ache the almond bite sew your
shadow sew your shadow
to my thick pink rim

Monkey

Dorothy waits in a motel by the airport watching Marlin Perkins on *Wild Kingdom*, pushes the bed hard against the wall, then next to the window, then back against the wall. She listens to Mahler, picks fuzz-pills off the orange bedspread, paces, eats a bag of *Corn Nuts*. He isn't going to show, she knows, tasted it that day on the phone when his voice got watery as if he had run into the bathroom to speak. It was all about *wing* and *tail*, how she traced the inverted *C*s on his back, cut the sutures with cuticle scissors. He wanted her to push the side of her hand into those long holes, through skin, muscle, tendon, until she touched the flat scapulas, the incisions were that clean, and later, he wanted her to kiss the spongy pad of scar tissue where the tail had been. The neon motel sign flicks on. Dorothy wipes her hands on her blue dress, smoothes it over her knees. She's pretty sure she won't see him again.

Swing

*I'm Cynthia Doyon. You are listening to The Swing Years
and   Beyond. The time is 12 midnight.*

Did you
did you
did you
consider the ravenous gulls
as you walked the dock at Portage Bay
behind the oceanography building?
(fry me cookie)
Did you
think, as I would have thought,
an easy cleanup, sluice the dock
with a hose, hose it down,
the university police prowler
flashing its weak blue light
as they gawked at your body,
your right hand skimming the water
as though you were about to go
for a swim?
Details are not forthcoming.
(fry me cookie)
Did you
put the gun to the side of your head
or in your mouth? Did you taste
the hole, did you lick that zero
with your oiled tongue?
You never returned my calls,
Saturday nights on Alki Beach,
cars and salt, the briny smell,
the instrumental version.
You never returned my calls.
(fry me cookie with a can of lard.)
Goodbye
goodbye
goodbye.

Burning Season

I was afraid of the rabbits. I wanted to tell you about horses,
how leather felt in my mouth, the musky barn taste.

You were my witness. You saw nothing. You could not describe
halter, hoof pick, bit or blanket. I wanted to tell you everything.

You faced the door as flames hissed and tumbled across
the grass. A clover-poisoned cow bellowed on her side.

I could not nurse her. I could not hold anything.
A nail pierced the sole of my soft boot

and the horses quaked in their stalls. I wanted you
to be my witness. I wanted you to listen.

I wanted you to see the russet crush of rabbits
pouring out as the fields burned.

Stabilimentum

The spider bite slings red into everything—
plum tomatoes dented, bent against
their stake, geranium blossom thick
with foamy bugs, the leather covered
Bible her father gave her at confirmation,
her name in gold, Christ's words in red.

She fingers the disk raised
under her left breast, a scarlet
throbbing coin. Her cotton shirt
rubs and rubs when she walks.
Perhaps a hot compress, ice, antiseptic,
a mouth pressed to the flamed edges
to suck, to soothe the heat, tongue licking,
licking, an animal cure.

The welt grows tight and perfectly round.
It is all she can think about—skin stretching
to accommodate, her fever, how the body
welcomes and closes around
what is given.

The Dance

Dreaming Patsy Cline

I stand so close to the microphone,
pomegranate lipstick smudges
the honeycombed case,
slide hands down my waist
along a flare of hips.
White satin sings against my palms.

Men watch my ass,
little girls in cowboy hats
think I'm too big, too bold.
My voice corkscrews from my body
like something wild tearing its way out
and their faces turn up to me,
and they are in love.

I lift two fingers,
touch the scars on my forehead,
nylon skin of my wig itching and hot.
The boys play too fast
on this sloped, uncertain stage.
I need a drink.
Pancake makeup thick in the lights
oils the creases around my mouth,
washes into my eyes.

I miss my sweet house,
babies pillowed in their beds.
My suitcase is packed: three dresses,
a bottle of gin,
gold lamé slippers
and a cigarette lighter
that plays Dixie.

Kit Kat Club

His sax is a Chinese puzzle
glazed in butter to crack and fry.
Reeds zisss, sting fingers, pinch
tongue, sizzle against skin
like Edith Piaf on amphetamines.

Big bottom girls cook,
tight pants slit up the side,
scat-bop-doowop sliding scale,
butter-tongued cats
plumped and creased in red capris,
toes squeezed in shoes
three sizes too small.

Sissy likes jazz, snaps her hips,
sax bends over Sissy's heat
creamed in butter, thighs pressed tight.

Sissy, Sissy, take me home

Cat yelps from stage.
Sax swings gold with juice and lip,
howling, howling
honey on that gilded hook.

St. Lucy

Lucy' legs bucked and pumped,
strained against the yellow dress
her father wove from silk with bits of bone
to press her ribs straight. He tightened a wool cap
to hold her hair itching against her skull.
No boys sniffed around Lucy's door—
she chose her narrow room,
sealed her ruby seam with wax,
bolted the candle to her palm.
Fortunato saw her first,
bartering fowl in the public square.
She circled and hexed the vendor's cart.
Her eye, he noticed, pulsed pink,
livid with dust and the reek
of market air. He told her she was beautiful
as gosling down.
Lucy spat at Fortunato's feet.
Charmed, he followed her home,
scratched and whined
let me break your chicken's neck,
pluck and boil, sweep pinfeathers
from the kitchen floor.
Ever her fathre's girl,
Lucy cut out her eyes,
arranged them on a plate,
served them up to the boy's
stammered plea.

Breakfast with Clara

I wonder how Clara Schumann felt
screwing Brahms behind Robert's back.
Did she dream of pulling her fingers
through Brahms' blonde hair
as she sat down to breakfast
spreading jam on black bread?

Robert glowers.
Songs glitter in Clara's brain like bees in a box,
brimming over, spilling onto the sun-washed table.
Even the curtains tremble
with deceit.

Her legs shift nervously under her morning dress,
fingers tap a milky tea cup.
Clara, stop tapping.

I would eat your music like a peach dear Robert,
and wear the stone in my button shoe
if only you would let me be.

Children hover in the nursery, voices tinny and chirping.
Robert's eyes twitch like lizard eyes,
his pallor green as the Rhein.

Caroline Pares Her Nails

This is how Caroline pares her nails, a tiny curved scissor glints in pink palm is how Caroline cuts the moony edge, gathers prim cuticle, orange stick-stickbug pushing back the fleshy rim is how Caroline creams her palms, callus to callus Caroline's pink palm, is how she paints her nails brush dipped in lacquer, sable smoothed flat against slick cell is how Caroline paints her nails, draws color cold, brings hand to mouth, touches paint with tip of pink tongue to taste to test if the nail is dry, is how Caroline paints her nails, is how Caroline pares her nails.

Cygnet

It is impossible to write a poem
about cygnet swans lazing south of the bridge
black and luminous under licorice necks.
Nor can I write of my dead neighbor's children
who hollow her garden to build a fence.
Tulip bulbs rustle their oniony hearts in panic.
This afternoon I guided my granddaughter's hand
as she painted a sunflower on the belly
of a ceramic plate amid the noise and snot
of toddlers mewling against their mothers.

This is not a poem's seed:
the bodies of swans languishing.
Tulips bend their wolf-heads against my hand
as children bright and cunning,
dig in the ground.

Chum

She writes in a room
that faces Piper Creek,
where salmon have returned
after twelve years.
He asks *what should I be
for Halloween?* knowing
she doesn't want to hear
his voice, his little whine.

*Be a car tearing off a bridge
at 80 miles an hour,* she says.
*Be a prosthetic hand, a crate of oranges
burning in Madrid, be Sylvia Plath,
a suture, an oboe, a swamp, a berry
in a duck's beak.*

You'll never sell your novel,
he laughs from the kitchen
finning his hands in a pan of dishwater.

She presses a pillow into her face,
pictures the house on the beach
she can never afford, sees herself
walking from room to room
dressed in copper silks,

knowing how, in winter,
when the moon is new,
she will lie on her side
above turbulent water,
dig a redd with her tail
as the male swims

back and forth, back
and forth above her,
staring into her fuchsia mouth,
her magenta mouth, her scarlet,
stretched, wide-open
blazing mouth.

Brazil Vesperæ
for Ron Jones

Dixit
He poached pears upright
in a copper pot. Drenched
in lemon juice and ginger,
their sugary clockworks uncoiled,
springs collapsed
at a terrible speed.

Confitebor
His wife asked if he dreamed
of Brasilia, the woman in bare feet,
toes perfect as pecans?
All that heat and his skin
like unleavened dough.

Beatus vir
He smoked brown cigarettes,
sold appliances at Sears,
fingers stained with shoe polish,
motor oil.

Laudate Pueri
With lips and tongue,
he named the sugary filigree,
the sensitive source.

Laudate Dominum
He loved sharp
knives, oiled and welcome
in wooden sheathes.

Magnificat
She fed him spindled
fish, wrapped his cut finger in linen
when he sliced a mango
in the shape of a star.
Blood seeped through white
like a mouse's heart pulsing
in a bowl.

Royal St. Charles

He stops on the street, shoes thick
with muck, the city leaking
up his legs, licks oyster juice
from his palm, slicks back his hair.
Boys with beer can lids
nailed to their sneakers tap dance
as he crosses St. Peter to Decatur,
hey mister, roll me!
they slouch into oozing brick walls
as he passes, the mud and drench
of river sluicing his skin.

Wrapped in a wet sheet, she watches
cartoons in the hotel, twists her hair
in knots, mutes the television
when sirens squeal nine stories down,
bites a spiced pecan, lets half fall to the floor.
She flattens her naked body
against the window, tries to press
through dripping glass.

The smell is deeper; vomit, the afterbirth
of swamp. An oak juts through water,
trunk larger than his house. He sees her feet,
pointed as a cat's ear, lips pruned
around a cigarette, the way she sucks
the smoke like stroking herself.
Air smudges a damp finger
under his shirt, lingers at nipple,
belly, buttons undone, trousers
loosened and huge around his legs.

The boys dance again or different
boys, a new corner, cunning faces,
cardboard boxes rattled with coins.
He stands in a doorway, pushes
his hands against the frame,
counts to one hundred, steps
out as his arms float away
from his body.

Repair

He bent to fix the track when his hair caught
in the metal jaw clamps of the roller coaster
Tremors   he simply lifted from his shoes
annoyed at the clicking   heard

                    carpet tacks
                         beetles
                    Glenn Gould

click   as his hair wound around the gears   carried
his body over Lake Coeur d' Alene   the floating green
golf course in its neon dress   the boardwalk
his grandfather's house on the hill   the Ford dealership

He realized he had a hole in his pants pocket
smelled fish frying at Lou's   worried   at the chicken he left
defrosting on the kitchen counter   his daughter   failing math

Oh how beautiful the geese in their tail   spin
near his mouth   how the swollen gears   arrowed
toward his house   his canoe leaning   length-wise
against the north side   all those Idaho winters   peeling
the exquisite paint   the whole lake swinging away

For My Son Who Doesn't Miss Me
Key West, 2002

Me, bobbing in the sea in my ridiculous hat.
Seven pelicans squatting on a beach-house roof, scratching their bellies.
Cats who own every street, fat on fried conch and sun.
Night-blooming jasmine, salt, beer.
A frigate bird swooping over my head for fish.
Palm trees dropping chartreuse pods in my coffee cup.
A bar rag from *Sloppy Joe's* and Hemingway's face
on everything like the Shroud of Turin, Hemingway
who bought a Ford from your great-grandfather in Ketchum
where they drank and hunted and killed a bear upon whose skin
you played as an infant, patting the big, sorrowful head, the oily fur,
with your hands.

Hurricane House

We make cigars on Elizabeth Street,
roll the leaves between palm and thigh
as the hurricane hums from the sea.
Pelicans start, turtles lift their heads
to watch the green, swollen sky.

Windows flex, fly west over
our heads. Wooden pegs squeal
in the walls. Scuttles wag
their tongues, rip from the roof.
We shake our petticoats and run.

The cigar maker's house shudders
from its stone, tumbles across
the cay, doors open like the wings
of a frigate bird. Work benches
fling splintered slats upward.

Chavetas whicker through thick air.
The gumbo limbo tree splits, bark
peeling in strips. We pull the braids
from our hair and dance, as frangipani
blossoms burst open on the fragrant lawns.

Flamingo

Audubon set his sights. Startled, the pink wing
broke open, stroked air across the water to Cuba,
legs tucked, sand lance flickering in curved beak,
mosca, lejos, lejos!

Audubon packed his pots, guns, brush
and wire, left for home without his prize.
A doctor brought the bird down,
packed it in rum, sent it by train

to Charleston where Audubon dried its tender
feathers with a tea towel, painted the great
bird — neck coiled, head in the reeds,
drinking, still at last, *silencioso.*

Angela Street

At Angela Street and Passover Lane
cemetery saints and the Virgin tilt
in limestone beds. Roosters peck
amid night-blooming jasmine.

I drink coconut milk by a stone carved
José Alvarez, Beloved Son, 1853,
the year yellow fever swallowed
the island's coral heart. A bicycle is propped

against a palm tree, the soil rich with toys,
beads, shoes, bones flung up by hurricanes.
I eat casabe bread and rice from the Cuban
market on Grinnell Street.

I wait with the *Garcías*, the *de Leons*, the *Vegas*.
I wait on Solares Hill for a cooling breeze.
I wait to see if the bicycle has a rider.

Divertimento

He's drawn to her professional tango
voice, honey-slick for a precise number
of minutes, an equation, a sequence,
an interlude to amuse, to divert himself.
Divertire, divertere, divertiss, devertir.

In between turns she watches the sky
for signs, cleans the chimney in case
he drops in, lights the fire, always
waits and tends the fire.
She is a rag soaked in gasoline.

She is instrumental, a chamber work
in several movements, hears Mozart
as owls fling themselves from linden
trees under magnetic influence.
He swings, an erratic compass needle.

He feints, admires the symmetry of her
breasts, her arched eyebrow, the timbre
of her voice singing arias from the bath,
Don Giovanni, all the blood running out.
Ebbi le mie ragioni. È vero?

Safety Training Film # 16

He enters her life, an unlocked
air hose, the kind they make
safety films about in the factory,
red rubber tube snaking around,
brass nozzle hissing. In these films,
a woman or a man loses an eye
or worse. Paramedics are called,
valuable hours wasted, inventory
stacks up, the economy fails.
This is what it's like. He makes
her come like Jesus but flinches
at her face, that stern mouth,
piggy eyes staring.
Once she broke a rib on the job.
Her breasts were taped and
it hurt to run for two years after.
She lies in bed, Schiaparelli
red nightgown tangled around her
throat just the way he likes it,
holds her rib, waits
for him to call.

Coda

The 7th brings night, the rest is rehearsal, tissue memory,
left hand strikes, lift, muscle tremble, open string, bow

arm swooping out. What language did you speak?
You never stopped — pathetique, serenade, romanza,

fingers, hands, throat. How could you forget, asleep
on the staff, fermata, the struck anacrusis?

I made you cry. I did not understand the cadence.
O Amadeus! O Schumann! O Brahms! O Ludwig!

drunk, scratching sums on the cupboard door. I believed
you, *dolce, dolce*, slipping along the timpani's copper rim.

I'm sorry. I'm sorry. I'm sorry.
I forgot to breathe.

The Cure

Music for Piano, 4 Hands

I stood in the kitchen, water, water
everywhere, cupboard door fallen,
plates broken, we cried,
        sugar   spilt   oil   spilt.

Music was there,   tremendous,
beautiful as fuck,   oh blonde fury,
it's about *that* day,   *that* one,
        bear witness.

One night Rayleen got drunk, fell asleep
with her glasses on   fell
asleep in her car,   fell asleep,
        no, no,   through the windshield.

Rayleen, who left a box of oranges on my porch,
Rayleen, who braided my hair, Rayleen,
who wrapped my wrists, Rayleen,
        who held me when I seized on the flightline.

I read it in a magazine when I was 12—
a girl buried alive, straw in her mouth to breathe.
I haven't felt right since, haven't felt what rang
        out, what rang out *that night*.

We wasted so much time. You pruned
the pear trees, set the sprinklers, lit
the smudge pots as the boy stepped
        down   stepped   down

into the lake. I flew   *flew!*
broke my rib on a limb as I   *flewflewflew*
across the orchard, caught
          his right foot in my left hand

just before he sank. You forgot to watch.
You forgot to use the key I passed you
in a kiss. You forgot
          what rode in my belly.

Forgive us our Ramblers, our Buicks,
our careless engines. Forgive us.
This is the broken window.
          This is the air rushing in.

Aperture
for Diane Arbus

You pressed thin fingers against jaws
and hats and hair and houses,
until real faces grim as Bible dogs
appeared in your lens:
mouths that poked out,
rubbery swollen tongues.

I was twelve when I saw them
at the Museum of Modern Art.
Nine foot high transvestites
pixilated in black and white,
the languid, sodden bodies
of carnival families you loved,
you loved, yes, you loved them,
each bump and twist and pocked pouch
of flesh.

You've been gone twenty years,
asleep in your red bath,
a negative about to turn.
New photos have been found—
the unbearable beauty of those children
who could never hide,
who were exactly what they seem
and there you are, Diane
simple and clean
as salt.

Comfort Food

When I heard you died
I thought of cabbages;
tight little heads in a row
bunched and green
and the salad we ate last April
when Julia plucked out
the blood ripe strawberries,
spun them on her tongue.

I cooked asparagus, walnuts,
silken, palm-heavy pears
speckled, dripping
toward your slow lung,
your tired, knobby spine.

Later I brought casseroles;
white sauce and baby peas
soaked in butter,
soup that snapped with tiny carrot fingers,
plump turnip hearts.

When you stopped eating
I still brought food,
placed chocolate animals in a pentagram
on your window sill
to keep the dark, sweet dream
at bay.

A User's Guide to the Interchangeability of Lips

1. Lap

Feed the feral cats who drink
from your swimming pool, swift
as little machines. Measure
the amount that can be carried
to the mouth in one lick or scoop
of the tongue. Load and fire
in safety, never in haste.
Break a teapot and float
the pieces to China.

2. Labium

Arrange snapdragons in a jar.
Open the beveled edge, the spout.
Always have a friend who works
in the hotel kitchen. Flow into,
draw the tongue over,
envelop entirely.

3. Embouchure

Say the word *prune*
while looking at yourself
in a mirror. Study the shape
of your lips, tongue and teeth.
Rub your stubbled jaw against
the mouthpiece of a French horn.
Now you know.
Now you know.
Now you know.

Sorrento

You ratchet everything
with the edge of your tongue,
make tidy sums of clothing,
wool, buttons
that rattle in a paper cup.

My arms fold like cranes.
I'm suddenly aware of commas
standing up, shouting
on my skin.

Oh! an afternoon in cotton sheets,
abalone combs slipped into my hair,
all the branches of your body
astonished in my hands.

Apothecary

Every morning she places pills in tiny saucers.
Cabbage Rose porcelain, a child's English tea set,
service for eight. She lines the plates on her mantle,
names each pill, tumbles them like prayer beads.

Valium, when wings are pinned, shoulder blades
compressed and dangerous.
Xanax untangles the burden of faces, butcher blocks, savage children.
She stacks Soma like pillows or dainty rounds of bread—

three at a time and a tepid bath slacken her skin.
Lithium for extreme unction, pinched afternoons
when her legs attack each other and she falls.
Codeine tightens teeth to jaw, brings animal dreams.

Percodan, the deepest swim through sheet, mattress,
box springs that cut her body like sugar cookies.
Zoloft and Paxil cure metallic insects,
unexpected weddings, religious ceremony.

Ritual completes her.
She pulls chair to fireplace, opens a book.
Her hands flicker like moths.
Her head is a burning church.

The Cellist Cut Her Hair

She moved to the country to raise goats.
Now she practices in the piggery,

mute on the bridge to muffle the tone.
Her baby squeals in a wicker basket,

drowning out Poulenc, Britten, Sebastian
Bach pounding away at his organ,

children plucking his sleeve, shoe buckle,
rotting lace that shows at the back of his wig.

Anna Magdalena whispers in the kitchen.
Everything is powdered

and reeks of dust. Turnips and parsnips
poke their noses into the earth.

Once, before a concert, she threw a cup of snow
at a window of the Rudolfinum in Prague.

In the evening she milks, hums a hornpipe,
knuckles swollen round as radishes.

Naxos

Ariadne with her growly
low-in-the-throat aria

Minotaur
bedchamber
bleat

Shouts at trees garden
ripe desert blooms

swallow
gristle
tongue

His furry head ridged
human horn

invent
stitch
stretch

She thumps the Bull's Blood
beet fisting through sand

requiem
savory
poison

Draws milk sustains the pedal
point like an organ

neglect
pendulous
circumstance

She has questions about *husbandry*
certain he will eat her alive

Yangshuo Quay

At night, my father's boat is strung with lanterns. I give him
a basket of pears, three dumplings wrapped in paper.

He presses his thumb to the top of my head for *goodbye*,
enters the Li River with his flock of tethered cormorants.

They fly out on their leashes, kites flickering against limestone.
The avu swim close, attracted to the bob and sway of lanterns.

The cormorants swoop, pluck, swing the fish in pouchy beaks,
thrash against the wooden collars that circle their throats,

trying to *swallow, swallow*. My father reels the birds in,
pulls the fish out of their mouths.

In the morning he walks to the village and I ride my bicycle.
He laughs when I stretch my arms out, then flap,

caw and squawk, stretch my neck to one side,
then the other, like the cormorant escaping its collar.

Nest

Dear heart, it's time. I've felt it for weeks,
and just this morning the barn swallows
returned to build their nest in the eaves,
flew 600 miles in a single day to find me
wading the reeds in Tadpole Pond.
Their split tails cut the air, orange throats
sucking up insects spring intended
for my garden. This is how we line
the nest; feather, horse hair, cotton.
This is how we catch with our mouths
in midair. This is how we return time
after time, voices cracking winter's
scab, voices humming, pitched
sideways like warmed paraffin. I'm not
afraid to say it. I never wanted this great
distance, all those miles ringing out.
Darling, my desire sings from mudslide,
bees frozen in the comb, magnolia lifting
her stingy pink fingers to heaven. I am
the clubfoot colt, the crooked lamb,
the cleft and bloody whelp, the spoon-
full of mice stillborn in the kitchen drawer.
I am the buck-toothed girl who waits,
at the fence, watching for spring's
terrible thaw.

Explaining the Kandinsky Tree House

(shh)

They climb the rope ladder into a nest
of cardboard and blankets.

He covers her mouth with his hand,
holds her   *(there.)*

She describes light through leaves, opaque,
viridian. Look, something new, he says,

a curved flame,
crimson, sprung from brown madder.
He holds it against her lips,   *(insists.)*

(shh, shh)

Her skin blazes carmine, terra oxide red.
Water, he says,   *(is never clear.)*

They bump the ladder up the sienna trunk,
alone, finally alone, breathing into each other.

She begins again:
the uniformity of green

rings out like a mad tuba   *(gold)*
green, green tea in hansa yellow

cups she has carried up,

tea   *(she has drunk too much.)*

She continues. White, she says,
ivory black outlines, primary, bright,
never mixed colors.

She is   *(full, very full, she has drunk too much.)*

She squats, his hand on her belly, his mouth
on her belly, staying her, staying her

            (shh, shh)   (mon père entend, écoute.)

She thickens herself into him, reaches up,
picks a pthalo green leaf to reveal
a slice

                              (of cobalt blue)

ultramarine blue, blue lake, blue
(rider)   sky.

Cha-no-yu

You washed your hands,
drew a jade parrot from
your sleeve as you knelt
at the tokonoma. Your
hair smelled of anise.
I had taken a lover
in another village.
My hand did not tremble
when I beat the tea
into froth. Your mouth
pulled down as you drank.
I gave you my Raku
pot, an English spoon,
a blood orange. You
dropped the parrot
in the snow when
you left.

Photographing Eva
for Sally Mann

When the greyhound, Eva, died, Sally skinned the dog,
buried the body under a pear tree. After fourteen months
she parted the soil with her hands, lifted the dog's bones.
The land, she said, *knows how to tend the dead.*

Sally arranged the rib cage in the shape of a boat.
A tibia standing alone absorbed light. She stroked
the narrow skull, scapula, femur, folded the hide,
the toast-point ears, fur limp as flannel. The dog's
nose pointed south, then east, camera swaying
on its tripod, heavy with wet colloid plates.

When the photographs were finished, Sally buried the bones.
Eva became part of the farm again, a trace of lean leg chasing
rabbit, snout lifted to catch the scent of falling snow.

Canning Pears With Fay

Summer slips its knot
with a jangle of bracelets
up Fay's arm as she peels
a pear with a knife, slices
the palm-heavy fruit in half,
scrapes the core with a spoon,
the kitchen thick with steam and sugar.

Each morning she walks the rows of trees,
hips bent wide, scratching bark,
the smudge pot's burning cough, the hiss
of sprinkler and horse's sweet muzzle.

Fay rubs her finger over tiny scars
where a child bit a new pear,
touches the brown-edged hole a bird
pierced with its beak to drink
the yellow meat.
She scoops and digs, drops the pear
in a bath of lemon juice and water,
slings the skins into a bucket.
Jars rattle in the kettle, amber shoulders
blistered and clean.

The orchard's children bleat in the cellar,
and Fay says, *I have baked twenty-one
thousand loaves of bread*, and her teeth clack
when she laughs, dishcloth shimmying
like a flag, like a wing, in her hands.

The house is green under eaves,
insects chewing wood, the lake still
as a fulcrum. The orchard brays
its terrible secrets and Fay lifts
the jars from their bath with rubber-tipped tongs,
and the lids begin to pop, and Fay swings
her face to the valley as summer bangles
its heat up her arms, all those jars of fruit
lining the shelves, shining like hearts.

What to do While Moving

1.
She jumped at the chance to drink a bit of Bengal dew,
pressed cheek against the raised lettering
of a Radio Flyer wagon, slammed knees into chin
to fit. Morning glory vines choked the wheels.
She demanded the mice pull her around the yard.
Paris, the cat, looked away, scandalized.

2.
A serial killer lurked in Paris's breath.
He lunged against tall grass, stalking,
knowing exactly what to do while moving,
the air itself wary as a cow at dawn, bellowing its need.
Sheep, too, startled as the kingfisher
slept in the cat's milky throat.

3.
Paris sang a bosky aire strutting along the fence.
His danger was becoming.
The woman was becoming Ophelia.
The secret of all carnivores is *red*.

4.
The moose thickened with poison.
She pocketed the antler's velvet
to decorate her Christmas tree
and spooned the rest over morning glories,
lost in the wood, hunting for lilacs
and morels to make a soup
to ward off visitors.

5.
The cat rubbed his musk against the ash tree, snaked
his tail around the trunk, beckoned to the woman
with his sly whisker, his creamy belly, his raspy
tongue. He spoke and was worshipped
with gifts of tobacco, butter and sweets.

Idiot Savant Caught by Surprise in a Lonely Time

I hope I hope I have not lost hope
watch wait woodpecker wood
thrush up the telephone pole
in the garden on hands and knees
await the evangelical fire
meaty thumb olive oil anointed
spirit-filled mud mulch
like a mink collar circles
the Rembrandt tulips.

You perch in the Russian olive tree wave brown branch
speckled wing lovely wing your mouth stuffed with berries
pout of ripe snowberries folded and folded in your secret
pouch a flag a rhizome in your mouth dangles its thick
red root we are rendered for a moment breathless we
are rendered without speech we are rendered.

I believe everything sleep with pictures
of saints under my pillow I *Hail Mary*
I *Our Father* thicket compost prune
dig water measure slick segmented
worm handsome bee hosannas
leafscud eggshell leftover
breakfast my kitchen's
salty crimes I carry the seeds
to you in my hand I carry
them in spite of beak in spite of bite
and sting in spite of winter and wife.

This is how you sing warble peck caw this is how you wake to find me your voice your spine against my spine that travels a V in the southern sky this is how you sing this is how you drop the berry into my mouth this is what you promise this is what you carry and I could no more hold you than I could hold the sea when it enters my back door I could no more contain you than I could contain the sudden dazzling lilt.

~

OTHER TITLES FROM RAVENNA PRESS

Harold Bowes: *If Nothing Else*

Denis Emorine: *No Through World*

Soren Gauger: *Quatre Regards sur L'Enfant Jesus*

Lynn Kozlowski: *Historical Markers*

Norman Lock: *Notes to "The Book of Supplemental Diagrams"
for Marco Knauff;s Universe*

Bryan McCarvey: *Temple Grounds*

M Sarki: *Little War Machine*

John Sweet: *Human Cathedrals*

and

Snow Monkey, an Eclectic Journal

Ravenna Press
PO Box 127, Edmonds, WA 98020
USA
http://www.ravennapress.com